Mrs Wilson

CW01651491

Will i[illegible]oday?

by Althea · pictures by Colin Robinson

Published by Dinosaur Publications

The weather is changing
all the time.
The day may start with sunshine
and end with a thunderstorm.

We want to know what the weather
is going to be like, so we can
put on the right clothes.
If it is going to rain we may
need our coats and boots.

The wind blows the weather
across the sky, taking clouds away,
or bringing other clouds which
may rain or snow on us.

Water evaporates from the sea and lakes, and rises up into the air. High up in the sky, tiny drops of water form and make clouds. It's like steam from a kettle.

When it is going to rain
the tiny drops of water in the clouds
join up to make big heavy drops
as they fall from the sky.

Some rain clouds bring thunderstorms too.
Thunder and lightning are caused
by electricity.
When you comb your hair
you make this sort of electricity.
Your comb can pick up tiny bits of
paper using this electricity.

When clouds make this electricity
there is a huge spark called lightning
which jumps between the clouds and the earth.
Thunder is the noise made by the spark.

When the storm has passed and
the sun shines on the rain
it makes a rainbow.

If it is very cold,
the warm air you blow out
is like fog. The water in your breath
mixes with cold air and makes
tiny drops of water.
Fog is made when warm moist air
mixes with cold air, or when
the air cools suddenly at night.

Sometimes the water in the air
falls on the ground as morning dew.
If it's very cold, the dew may freeze
and make a frost.

Black ice forms when rains falls on very cold roads.
It can be dangerous to motorists.
Water in puddles and ponds may also freeze
and turn into ice when it's very cold.

When it's very cold, the water droplets
from the clouds may freeze together
and fall out of the sky as snow or hail.

For some people it is very important
to know what the weather is going to be like.
Ships may need to change direction
to avoid a storm.
Aeroplane routes must be organised
to avoid storms too.

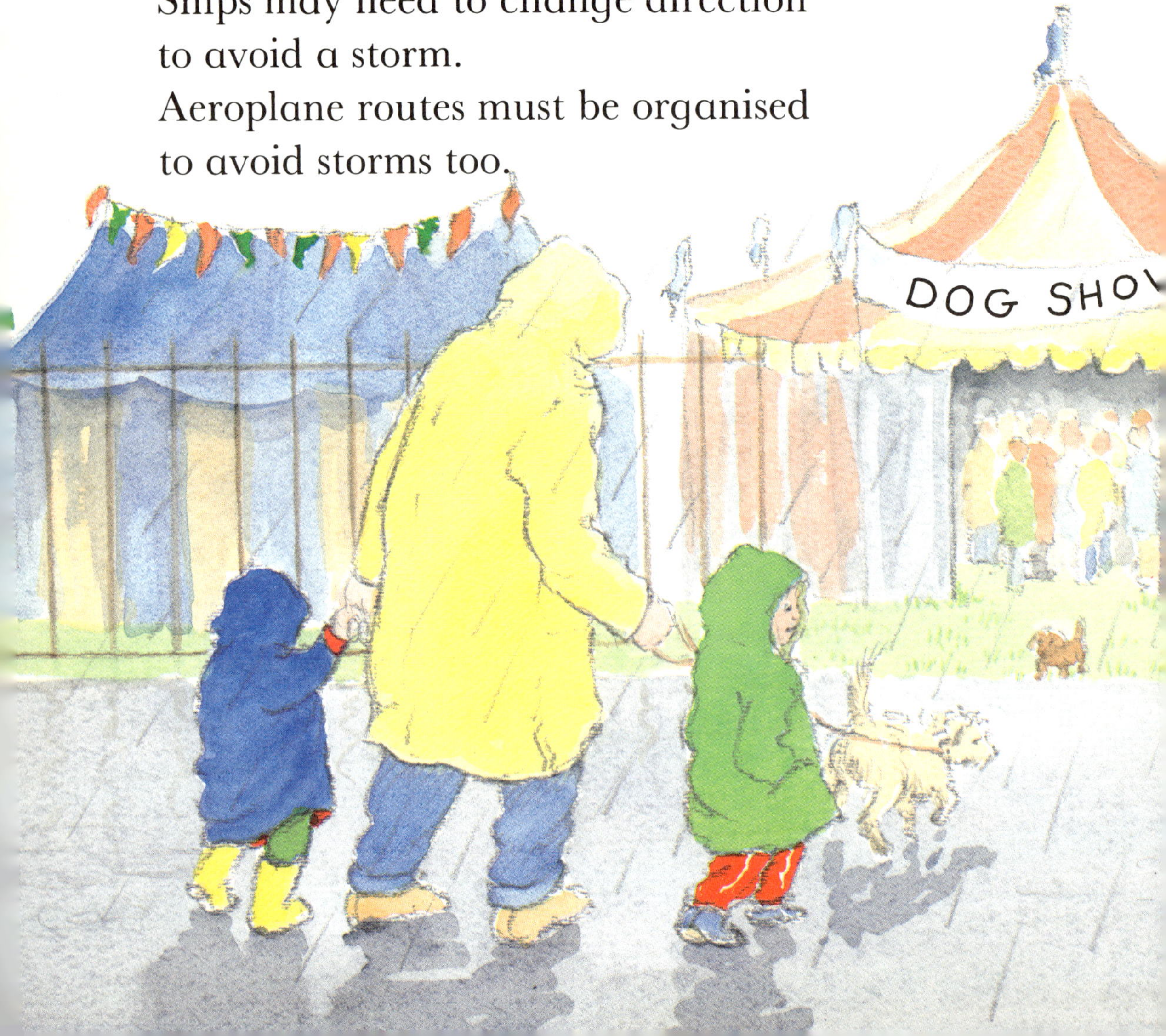

People planning fêtes or parties want to know if they can hold them outside, or if a tent will be needed. Farmers need to know when it will be dry enough to cut their crops.

Sometimes rain is badly needed, especially in hot parts of the world. Reservoirs, lakes and rivers can dry up and then crops, animals and people are short of water. This is called drought. Sometimes people pray for rain or do rain dances when this happens.

Scientists are experimenting with ways of making it rain by flying above the clouds and scattering them with a chemical powder to encourage the water in the clouds to form rain drops. This doesn't always work.

Weather forecasters try to tell us what the weather will be like for the next few days.

They study all the information
they receive. People on ships and
aeroplanes radio in weather reports.
The weather forecasters send up
balloons to check on wind speeds.
Satellites send down pictures of clouds
moving around the earth.
Computers help to forecast the weather too.

Many country people believe
they can forecast the weather
around them by watching the sky
and looking at nature.
Some flowers close their petals
before it rains.

There are lots of sayings about
the weather like, "red sky at night,
shepherd's delight", or "rain before
seven, fine before eleven."
How many others do you know?

"Rain from the East,
Will last three days at least."

"Ne'er cast a clout,
Before May is out."

"March winds and April showers,
Bring forth May flowers."

We want fine weather for our holidays, but gardeners and farmers may be needing rain to make plants grow.

The weather is never right for everybody, perhaps that is why people are always talking about it.

Text copyright © Althea 1988
Illustrations copyright © Colin Robinson 1988
All rights reserved
Published by Dinosaur Publications
8 Grafton Street, London W1X 3LA

Dinosaur Publications is an imprint of the Children's Division, part of the Collins Publishing Group

Printed by Warners of Bourne and London